The Party

Thea Franklin
Illustrated by Betina Ogden

Rigby

A Harcourt Achieve Imprint

www.Rigby.com
1-800-531-5015

The clowns are here.

The hats are here.

The balloons are here.

The friends are here.

The games are here.

The pizzas are here.

The cupcakes are here.

The presents are here!